Winston Churchill

윈스턴 처칠

Biography Comic
who? ⑮ Winstone Churchill

개정판 1쇄 인쇄 2014년 3월 5일
개정판 1쇄 발행 2014년 3월 10일

글 강민희
그림 크레파스
번역 채드 워커
감수 김수희
펴낸이 김선식

책임편집 이유미 **디자인** 박효영
콘텐츠개발팀장 김선영 **콘텐츠개발팀** 박효영, 이유미, 김선민, 조서인
마케팅본부 이상혁

펴낸곳 스튜디오 다산 **출판등록** 2013년 11월 1일 제414-81-37694
주소 경기도 파주시 회동길 37-14 3층
전화 02-702-1724(기획편집) 02-703-1725(마케팅) 02-704-1724(경영관리)
팩스 02-703-2219 **who클럽** cafe.naver.com/dasankids
종이 월드페이퍼(주) | **인쇄** (주)현문 | **제본** 광성문화사

ISBN 979-11-5639-037-4 (14740)

who?
Winston Churchill
윈스턴 처칠

글 **강민희** | 그림 **크레파스** | 번역 **채드 워커** | 감수 **김수희**

Dasan Kid

Winston Churchill

British prime minister, November 30, 1874 ~ January 24, 1965

Winston Churchill did not have a very happy childhood. His father, who was the Minister of Finance, and his mother, who enjoyed socializing with aristocrats, were too busy to spend much time with him. Young Winston was a troublemaker who caused his family to worry.

His family had high expectations of him as the grandson of John Spencer-Churchill, the seventh Duke of Marlborough. But his grades were bad and he even had a speech impediment, causing his classmates to make fun of him.

But once Winston would decide to do something, he would persevere and work hard until he accomplished it. For example, he worked day and night to correct his speech impediment which he had had since he was young. He read and memorized many books and searched for famous speeches and practiced them. As an adult, Churchill would be recognized as an outstanding speaker.

Churchill wanted to join the military and serve his country, but he failed the entrance exam to the Royal Military College twice and barely passed the third time. After graduating the College with top grades, Churchill became a war correspondent and witnessed some intense battles. He became captured as a prisoner of war in the Boer War, but then escaped and planted hope in the hearts of the British people.

During World War I, Churchill served as the Minister of Munitions. When World War II began, he led the nation, appointed as the Prime Minister. To people who had lost hope, Winston Churchill moved their hearts with his speeches and planted in them the courage to face the war and the belief that they would win. And through his superior leadership, he led them to victory in the war.

He was also an outstanding writer, receiving the Nobel Prize in Literature for The Second World War, a book about his war experiences. But most of all, Winston Churchill is an international leader who was highly respected for the strong leadership he demonstrated during the war.

윈스턴 처칠

영국의 총리, 1874년 11월 30일 ~ 1965년 1월 24일

처칠은 어린 시절 그리 행복하지 못했습니다. 재무 장관을 지냈던 아버지와 화려한 귀족 생활을 즐겼던 어머니는 늘 바빠 처칠의 곁에 있어 주지 못했고, 말썽꾸러기였던 처칠은 집안의 걱정거리였습니다.

제7대 말버러 공작 존 스펜서 처칠의 손자였던 윈스턴 처칠에게 건 가족들의 기대는 컸습니다. 하지만 성적도 나쁘고 말을 더듬는 습관까지 있었던 처칠은 친구들에게 놀림받기 일쑤였습니다.

하지만 처칠은 한번 결심한 건 끝까지 포기하지 않고 노력했습니다. 어린 시절부터 계속된 말더듬는 습관을 고치기 위해 처칠은 밤낮으로 노력했습니다. 책을 많이 읽고 또 외우고 유명한 연설문을 찾아 읽고 연습하는 노력 끝에 처칠은 훗날 뛰어난 연설가로 인정받게 되었습니다.

군인이 되어 나라를 위해 일하고 싶었던 처칠은 육군사관학교 입학 시험에 두 번이나 떨어진 끝에 세 번 만에 겨우 합격하게 되었습니다. 육군사관학교를 우수한 성적으로 졸업한 처칠은 실전 경험을 쌓기 위해 종군 기자가 되어 치열한 전쟁터를 경험합니다. 보어 전쟁 중에 처칠은 포로로 잡혔다가 탈출해 영국 국민들에게 희망을 심어 줍니다.

제1차 세계 대전에서 군수 장관으로 활약했던 처칠은 제2차 세계 대전이 시작되자 수상에 임명되어 나라를 이끕니다. 희망을 버린 사람들에게 처칠은 연설을 통해 사람들의 마음을 움직여 전쟁에 맞설 수 있는 용기와 이길 수 있다는 믿음을 심어 주었습니다. 그리고 처칠은 탁월한 리더십으로 전쟁을 승리로 이끌었습니다.

전쟁 당시 경험을 담은 『제2차 세계 대전』으로 노벨 문학상을 받은 뛰어난 작가이기도 했던 처칠은 전쟁에서 보여준 뛰어난 리더십으로 존경받는 세계적인 지도자입니다.

이 책을 만든 사람들

글 · 강민희

어린이들에게 도움이 되는 학습 만화를 만들기 위해 노력하는 젊은 작가입니다. 어릴 적 재미있게 읽은 책이 평생의 꿈을 바꿀 수 있다는 사명감으로 더욱 감동적이고 기억에 남을 만한 이야기를 만들기 위해 노력하고 있습니다.

그림 · 크레파스

어린이들을 위해 새롭고, 재미있고, 즐거운 이야깃거리를 만드는 만화 창작 집단입니다. 세상을 바꾼 인물들의 삶을 통해 어린이들이 희망찬 미래를 만들어가길 바랍니다. 작품으로 『지식 똑똑 경제 리더십 탐구-긍정의 힘』, 『why? 서양 근대 사회의 시작』, 『why? 세계대전과 전후의 세계』 등이 있습니다. 이 책은 이준형 작가님이 그림을 그리셨습니다.

번역 · 채드 워커(Chad Walker)

미국 텍사스 오스틴에서 심리학과 일본어를 전공했습니다. 일본으로 건너가 10년 간 살았고 이후 한국과 중국을 오가며 한 · 중 · 일의 동아시아 문화를 비교 연구하고 있습니다. 현재는 연세대학교 국어국문학과 박사 과정 중에 있습니다. 옮긴 책으로 『한국어 교육을 위한 한국어 연어사전』, 『한국인의 가치 문화』, 『속성 한국어』 등이 있습니다.

감수 · 김수희

연세대학교에서 역사를 전공했습니다. 이후 한국뿐 아니라 일본, 미국에서 한국어, 일본어, 영어를 가르쳐 왔으며 부모를 위한 영어교육용 책을 썼습니다. 영어교육채널 EBSe '엄마표 영어특강'에서 강의를 하며 홈스쿨, 알파벳과 파닉스, 다차원 테마 영어 수업 기법을 알리고 있습니다. 전국 각지에서 어린이 영어 교육에 대한 강연을 하며 창의적이고 열정적인 교수법으로 영어를 배우고자 하는 어린이와 부모들에게 많은 도움을 주고 있습니다.

Winston Churchill

Winston Churchill won the Nobel Prize in Literature in 1953. What is the title of the book?

a. *A Farewell to Arms*
b. *The Second World War*
c. *War and Peace*

Answer: b

Contents

01 The Royal Troublemaker

 Track 01 ▶

Blenheim Palace, 1874.

I'm not due for two more months, and there's no way I could miss such a splendid party!

This is a wonderful ball you're throwing, but shouldn't you take some rest?

Oh!

Madam!

My stomach hurts. Let's leave quietly so we don t spoil the party.

Winston Churchill was the child of Lord Randolph Churchill, the third son of John Spencer-Churchill, 7th Duke of Marlborough, and American Jennie Jerome.

The Churchills were a distinguished family who had produced a number of famous politicians.

At that time in England, the sons of most families of royal lineage were raised by nannies. Winston was no exception.

You've got to get up.

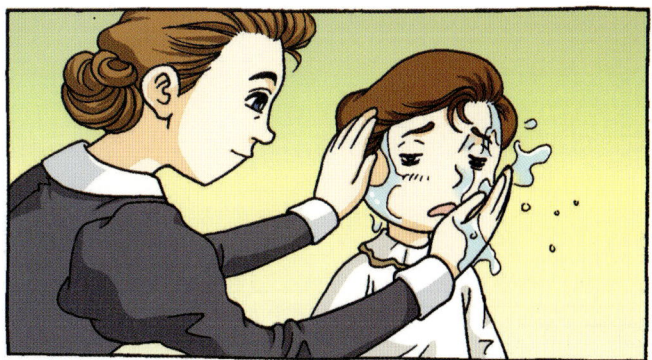

Now it's time to go to breakfast.

Has Father already gone to work?

He's in his study.

Really? I'll go see him then!

But I'll take you to see him later.

No, I'll go now!

Sorry, Winston, but you've got to have your breakfast first.

No! I'll go see Father first.

Winston!

Winston's father, Lord Randolph Churchill, was a well-respected politician who also worked as Finance Minister. It was therefore hard for him to spend a lot of time with his son.

Father!

Long time no see! My, how you've grown.

Aren't you working today?

They finally gave me a holiday.

KNOCK KNOCK

Who could that be? Wait just a moment.

But we just started playing...

So now can we play together?

Why yes, we can!

KNOCK KNOCK

Uh?

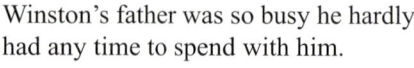

Winston's father was so busy he hardly had any time to spend with him.

Oh,

Mum's staying home today.

I've got to look my best today.

Wow, she's so pretty.

Yes, that's perfect!

To Winston, his mother was like a shining star. Although he loved her dearly, she always seemed at a distance, shining far away out of his reach.

With his father always busy and his mother always attending parties, neither of them had much time to spend with Winston. Winston thus spent a lot of time alone as a child.

Present for ya!

Ahhh!

Perhaps that was the reason why Winston became a stubborn prankster.

20

Someone must have dropped it down from above!

Hahaha! My sides are aching.

I bet she's long gone by now.

Oh!

Thus was Winston's first encounter with the new nanny, Mrs. Everest.

Hello, Winston.

Uh!

Even though the Churchill household was very strict, Winston was a troublemaker who never listened to his nanny.

Surely she can't find me here.

Ha! You think I can't go to the market just because you tell me not to?

All I gotta do is sneak out. Heh heh.

Wow, so many people.

I just realized I haven't had lunch.

GRRR

That sure looks tasty.

Mummy!

Mummy, a present for you!

Oh my, how beautiful!

That's it!

I'm gonna pick some flowers to give to Mum, too.

24

Winston!

Where did you go? I've been looking all over for you!

Um, I'm not telling.

Oh dear, Winston! Why are your clothes so dirty?

I went to pick you some flowers.

Thank you for that, but we've got lots of flowers in the garden. So next time you don't need to go out and get all dirty.

Um, okay.

Anyway, you can't go around looking like that.

Nanny, I think a bath is in order.

Ma'am, it's time to go.

Oh my, we'll be late to the party. Winston, have your bath and be a good boy.

Mum!

CLOP

CLOP

26

Such a young boy, poor thing.

WAAAAH

Mrs. Everest gave troublemaker Winston the love he longed for in his heart. Slowly, Winston began to open up to his nanny, who always cared for him.

02 · I Hate Studying!

And on that night,

the soldiers

Wow!

Boom! Went the cannons!

Really?

Grandpa, you're really brave!

Hahaha!

I see Winston quite likes war stories.

The general confronted the enemy and ordered his soldiers to attack.

And then they surrounded the enemy.

Wow, that's amazing!

Isn't it? War stories are so interesting.

It's so great to be able to protect one's country!

When I grow up and become a great soldier, I'll protect you, Nanny!

Winston detested studying. When it was time to meet the tutor, he would run away, only to be forced back to study by his nanny.

Why do I have to study?

Surely nobody can find me here!

So you've been hiding here, I see. You can't run away!

Ah!

The teacher has already been waiting a long time.

No, let me go!

Is Winston doing okay with his studies?

Well, um...

Does he have some sort of problem?

Let's just say he's still at the age when play takes precedence over study.

I need you to give me an honest assessment of my son's progress.

His reading is poor, and he's having trouble understanding addition and subtraction.

It seems he's not cut out for study.

Sending him to school should help, so let's give that a try.

As soon as he turned eight, Winston was enrolled in the very strict and conservative St. George's boarding school.

Winston, this is your new school. A lot of famous people have studied here.

Mum, I wanna go home. I don't wanna go to school.

Are you nervous about being around all the other students? Are you trying to disappoint me?

No, ma'am.

Mum! Visit me on weekends!

Darn!

So I'm stupid because I stammer?

Just wait!

I'll make sure they never call me a stammerer again!

Winston read books out loud in front of a mirror to improve his pronunciation.

Had t-t-ta en his last l-l-love, no, leave, of the w-w-weeping m-morn,

R-r-rose-ch-ch-cheeked Adonis hied him to the ch-ch-chase, h-h-hunting he loved.

Wow, is it already morning?

38

However, despite his efforts, young Winston still struggled with subjects other than reading. St. George's was a very strict school that practiced corporal punishment based on its students' marks.

Arms out!

Yes, sir.

Winston Churchill.

Step forward, please.

Why on earth do we have to study Latin?

You know why I've called on you, right? Follow me.

41

43

I've disgraced Father. I'm so horrible.

It's not your fault, Winston.

Look at these wounds. That teacher really went too far with the striking. They're still kids.

I had heard St. George's was strict, but I had no idea.

Ma'am, if this continues Winston won't be able to handle it. Maybe you could transfer him to another school?

I'll have to look into other schools.

Winston was transferred to Brighton, which had a freer, more relaxed atmosphere. His class marks, however, remained poor.

Winston's parents worried about his school performance.

Well, I'm really worried. I don't see any sign of progress at all.

And I had expected him to go to Oxford to study law and take my place.

That's probably not going to be possible given his marks.

I really worry about his future.

It's a real disappointment that our family name could produce such a poor student.

Upon graduating from Brighton, Winston now had to pass the entrance exams to prestigious schools if he wanted to follow his parents' wishes.

I don't know a single answer.

Everyone's writing so much.

Latin got the best of me in the end.

Now who could have turned in a blank answer sheet?

Winston Churchill? Isn't that the son of Lord Randolph Churchill, Chancellor of the Exchequer?

This is odd for a Chancellor's son.

Hm, except for Latin and Mathematics, he did fine on the other subjects.

Hmm.

Thanks to the headmaster's consideration of all the circumstances, Winston was admitted to Harrow School. Those around him now expected big things from this Chancellor's son.

Him, it's him!

Really? That's the son of the Chancellor of the Exchequer?

Yep.

Okay, just promise me you'll put a little more effort into studying Latin.

Latin's not worth it. However, I'll do my best in subjects I like. Won't that work?

Even at Harrow, Winston continued to work on his pronunciation.

So many things to do I've lost track of time.

Who could be up at this hour?

Death pursues the man who flees.

Winston, what are you doing at this time of night? It's late.

Is that you, Father? I'll go to bed after just a bit more.

KNOCK

KNOCK

Winston never gave up, and his perseverance and patience paid off.

Next, Winston Churchill will recite a poem from ancient Rome.

Heh heh. This should be good.

What a sight it will be if he stammers and pronounces the words wrong.

HEH HEH HEH

It...

...it is sweet and honorable to die for one's country.

Death pursues the man who flees,

Huh?

Looks like he practiced. But that's to be expected for the first few lines.

Right! From now it should start getting interesting. It's time to enjoy ourselves!

...spares not the hamstrings or cowardly backs of battle-shy youths.

What? Why doesn't he stammer?

I can't believe it! Perfect pronunciation!

He's doing quite well.

Indeed.

Surely he didn't memorize the whole poem?

But there's still more to go. Here comes the last part.

03 Dreaming Big with Toy Soldiers

Track 23 ▶

55

I want to lead real soldiers to battle.

Risking one's life to protect one's country is such an honor.

But being a soldier is not all fun and games, you know. It's a tough job.

Father, I can handle it.

It would be nice if you took after me and became a politician.

To become a politician I have to have good marks. But I don't.

Oh, you were aware of that.

Yes, Father.

It won't be easy, but you might be able to enter the Royal Military Academy to fulfill your dream.

Really? Then I'll do my best!

Track 25 ▶

Winston studied harder than he ever had before to get into the prestigious Royal Military Academy.

Winston, are you going to study during our school vacation, too?

If I'm to enter the Royal Military Academy I have to keep studying even at the expense of sleep.

The exam is not that far away. Are you confident?

I can do anything once I set my mind to it. I will get accepted!

Yes, I know you'll do well.

However, Winston failed his first attempt at the entrance exam.

I gotta good feeling about this. I just know my name's on the list.

Okay, so where is it?

There must have been a mistake.

What!

Will Hunting

kiper | William Shakespeare

Winston Chele

It's not here!

Surely I didn't fail!

Winston resolved to devote himself to his studies once again.

Winston took the exam again, only to fail for a second time.

I've failed again!

How can this happen? I studied so hard!

Winston, how did your exam go?

...

Apparently he failed this time as well.

At this rate he probably won't be able to become a soldier.

He must be devastated. I've got to go talk to him.

Just because you failed this time doesn't mean you will again. However, if you give up now, you'll lose any chance you had to succeed. You become a failure the instant you give up.

Muster the courage to take the test again, and do it!

Ohhh.

BAM

Father...

I had no idea Father really believed in me. What am I doing?

Father's right. I'm the Winston Churchill who never gives up. I'm going to fight this to the end.

Winston made the decision to sit for the exam one final time.

While preparing for the exam, Winston spent any free time he had sitting in the public gallery of the House of Commons, listening to his father's speeches.

We can't let that motion pass in the form Member Flynn has submitted it.

But shouldn't we hear the opposition's argument first?

This motion must pass legislation!

Let's hear what the citizens have to say!

No different from politicians, soldiers are also indispensible to a country.

That's it! I'm going to become a great soldier who fights for his country.

I'm determined to become a son my father no longer has to be ashamed of.

04 In the Midst of War

Track 31 ▶

Winston didn't give up, and was finally accepted into the Royal Military Academy. Starting his studies as a cavalry office candidate, he attended all of his classes with great interest.

When crossing a place like this with hills, you must use extreme caution, as this type of terrain is easy for the enemy to use as an ambush.

Your decisions will determine the fate of all the soldiers under your command.

Winston was very successful at the Royal Military Academy. In 1894, he graduated with honors.

I will now announce the honor students.

William Tail.

Aye!

Winston Churchill.

Aye!

To think I could graduate with honors! Father will be so proud!

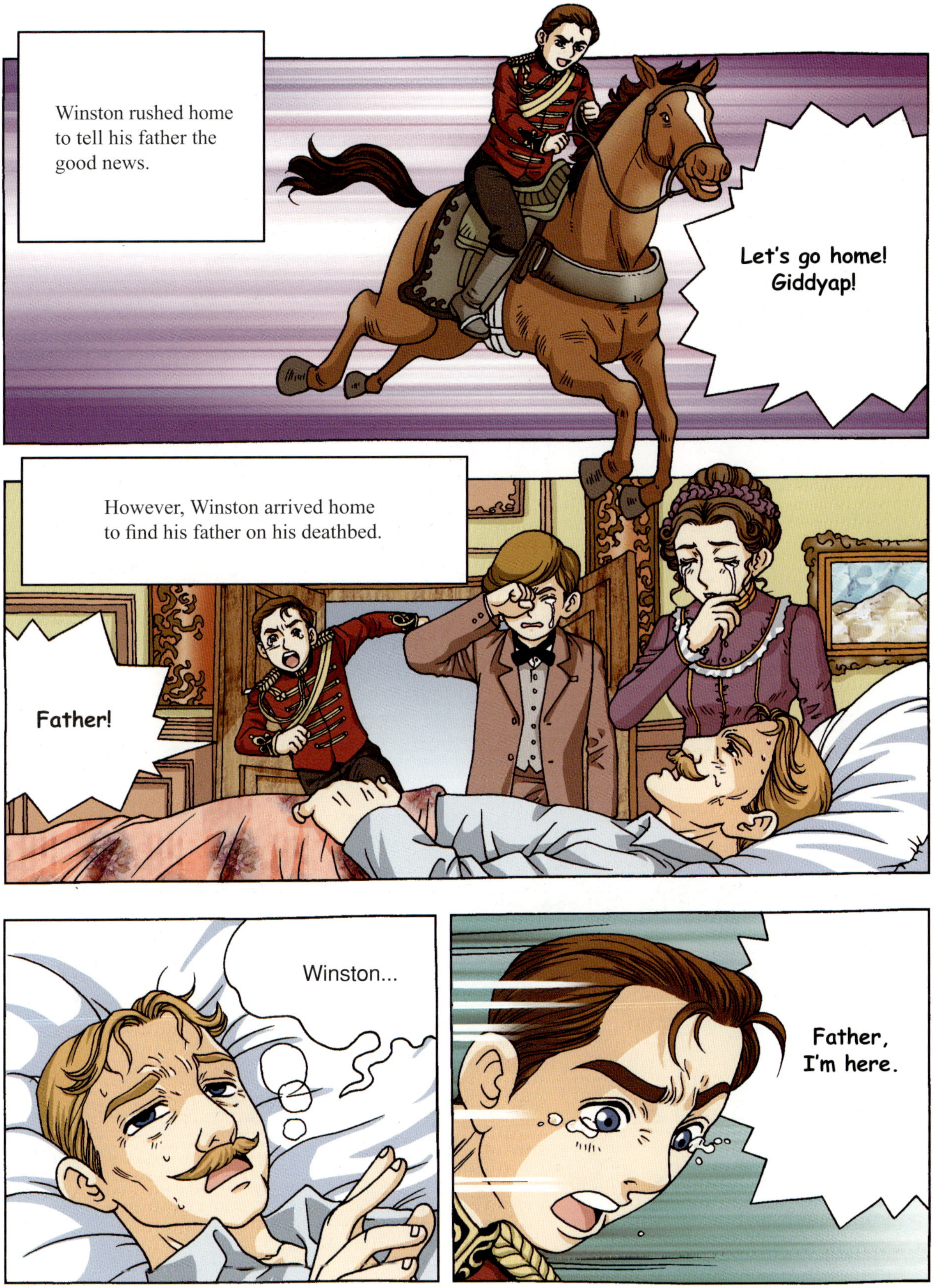

Winston rushed home to tell his father the good news.

Let's go home! Giddyap!

However, Winston arrived home to find his father on his deathbed.

Father!

Winston...

Father, I'm here.

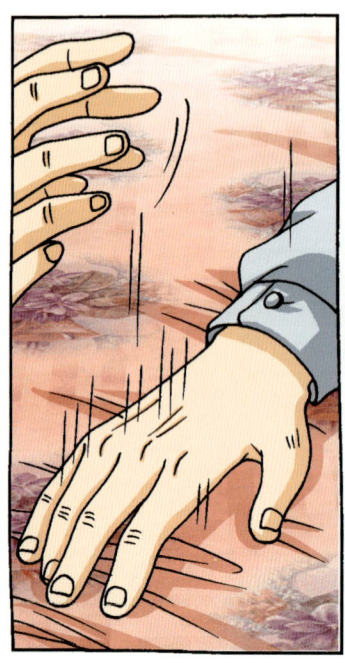

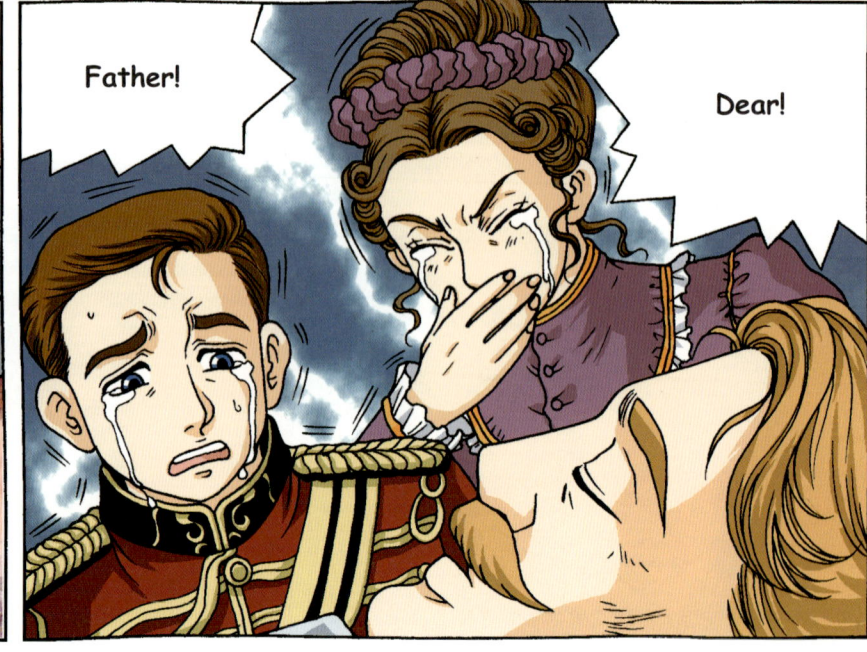

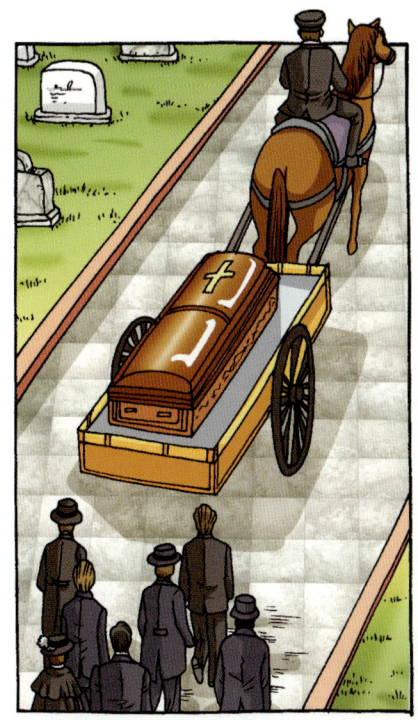

Whose footsteps
am I to follow now?

I've worked so hard to make Father proud.

Why couldn't he have held on just a little longer?

In February of 1895, Winston was commissioned as a Second Lieutenant in the 4th Queen's Own Hussars, and had to depart while still mourning his father's death.

I'm determined to become a great soldier that Father can be proud of.

In 1896, Winston's unit was ordered to go to India. India was a very important British colony, and therefore British soldiers had to serve duty there for a number of years.

I can't believe it! I thought we would be sent to real warzones as soon as we became soldiers.

Is it acceptable for a soldier not to have a single real combat experience?

What's wrong with not being sent off to war? It's better than being killed.

If war were to break out today, our army would suffer greatly. Soldiers have to directly experience a warzone.

Well, you're the exception. Most would rather not go off to the battlefield even if they were paid to go. But you, you want to go.

Is there no way we can directly experience war here? We've got to get experience before we leave for India.

But there hasn't been a war on British soil for over ten years.

But there are other countries having wars.

Come to think of it, Cuba's in the midst of war right now.

Although the war in Cuba was completely unrelated to England, Winston wanted to go to Cuba at all costs. To do so, he decided to become a war correspondent.

Is it true? Are you really going to Cuba?

My, how news travels fast.

Are you crazy? Cuba's in the middle of a war. What are you thinking, trying to go there?

Do you think it's acceptable for me to stand here as a general with no warzone experience?

Who's going to take orders from a general who's never stepped foot on a battlefield?

So you think you can just go off to a warzone? Officers are supposed to lead their troops from a safe location.

I've got to see the real thing before I can gain the trust of our troops. I've already signed up to go as a war correspondent.

You could be killed!

I'm aware of that. But nobody can make me change my mind.

So stubborn!

The Cuban independence army was fighting the Spanish using guerilla warfare tactics from secret forest locations.

The Cuban independence forces would ambush the Spanish soldiers, fire their guns, and then flee. Therefore it was impossible to predict when or from where they would attack.

Wow, this is so refreshing! How long has it been since we've bathed?

It's definitely been a while since we've been able to relax like this.

You're dirtier than the ground itself!

Hahaha!

By the way, have you written any good articles yet?

Not yet, because we still haven't seen a real warzone.

I don't know if I'd call that reckless or brave, but don't you think you should consider your safety first?

Not this again. Let's just say I'm different.

I'm ashamed to be a war correspondent who can't carry a gun and fight.

Well, you'll have something to write about before too long.

Are you saying the enemy's close by?

It's not certain, but I heard they might attack this evening or tomorrow morning.

This place where we're swimming is said to be safe, so enjoy it while you can, because tomorrow we won't have such luxury.

Thanks for the update.

The sight of a fellow soldier with whom he had spent so much time die right before his eyes was unbearable to Winston.

Tom, Tom! Answer me! This can't be happening. You can't die this way!

War was no longer the exciting experience he had read about in books at school.

Why did this happen? Why?

84

Why do we risk the one life we have by going to war only to wind up killing each other?

When you find the answer to that one, tell me.

Why do they have to die...

The smell of gunpowder and blood filled the air of the battleground along with the groans of the injured soldiers.

This is the true meaning of war.

The question of how to prevent the sacrifice of innocent lives in war continued to haunt Winston from the time he served as a war correspondent until he was to depart for India in 1896.

But the answer always eluded him. Figuring he might find the answer if he learned more about war, he spent all of his remaining time studying.

I can't make any progress, no matter how much I read.

05 .The Great Escape

 Track 01 ▶

Winston was still seeking the answers to his questions about war when the Boer Wars erupted. These battles began when Britain tried to recolonize the Boer Republics, which had temporarily become independent from British rule.

There's still no answer no matter how I think about it.

In 1899 Winston was dispatched along with the army to South Africa, where he rode a train with armed soldiers on scouting missions.

Nothing unusual here!

Excellent! Stop the train and report to headquarters.

Yes, sir!

The Boer soldiers are attacking!

Start the train!
No, attack!

Pardon?

Please calm down!
If combat drags on here,
we'll all be wiped out!

In that case,
what should
we do?

We've got to get the
train moving and escape.
I'll separate the derailed
car, and you command
the troops.

First we've got
to detach the
freight car!

Depart!

Hurry and board the train!

Oh no!

Stop briefly in front of that bridge!

What? If we don't leave quickly the Boers may catch up with us.

We have to save the remaining troops. If I'm not back soon then go ahead and leave.

Yes, sir.

This is my only chance!

Got it!

Hey! The Britain has escaped!

Quick, find him!

Winston took advantage of the Boer's careless surveillance and made his escape.

How much farther could it be?

The freight car. I'll have to hide in there.

Daybreak. I can't escape when it's light outside. The Boers will see me.

I'll have to hide until sundown.

99

There's a reward out for you.

!

There's only one man in these parts that won't turn you in—me. I'm British, too.

Heaven is truly on my side.

While Winston was busy escaping and trying to return to England, news of his escape was making big headlines back home.

The people of England, numbed by war, heard of Winston's escape and began following his story.

They say the war correspondent Churchill has escaped from the P.O.W. camp in Pretoria.

Extra! Extra!

That evening, Winston boarded a boat bound for England.

Ah, I'm finally back home, safe and sound.

There's Winston Churchill!

Churchill's returned!

What's all this?

Upon his safe arrival back in England after escaping from the P.O.W. camp, Winston was greeted with a hero's welcome.

YAY

HOORAY!

06 The Principled Politician

CD2 Track 08 ▶

Although Winston had become a hero back home in England, he still could not forget the horrible things he had experienced as a prisoner of war.

I just knew I was going to die!

The nightmares never cease. I can't imagine the horrible things the other soldiers must be going through back in the battlefield.

Winston recalled memories of his father.

What should I do?

That's it! A war is decided by a country's government.

I must follow in my father's footsteps and become a politician!

Winston had actually run for public office before, back in July of 1899, before the start of the Boer Wars. However, without a clearly stated platform, he was unsuccessful.

In which constituency do you plan to run for office?

I'm thinking of running in Oldham.

Isn't that where you ran and lost last time? Why there of all places?

Just think of how nice it will be to win where I've previously lost.

The more difficult the challenge, the greater the joy of winning.

I see you haven't lost your sense of adventure even after coming so close to death.

I wouldn't be Winston Churchill if I didn't love a challenge!

One can't drink a bitter cup of defeat twice. I've got to win at all costs.

I'll practice my public speaking using the speeches Father used to read.

Hmm.

We pray for the realization of freedom across our land!

Oh!

I bes -eech you!

Winston had become famous as a former P.O.W. of the Boer army. People liked him because he symbolized courage and hope.

Winston ran for Parliament in the same constituency where he had previously been defeated, only this time he won.

HOORAY!

YEAH

YAY

At the age of 25, newly elected Parliament member Winston became a member of the Conservative Party, which had also been his father's party.

I'm following in Father's footsteps.

Even if his opinion on an issue opposed that of his own party, he would stand firm without hesitation.

112

Nonetheless, the government must also understand a few things. If the current war continues, there will be even more danger and suffering.

The current government must increase it's tolerance. It must work to ensure the end of this war, by creating a policy to grant the Boers fair rights and freedom.

Winston spoke true to his beliefs. Even if his opinion was critical of his own party, he never compromised.

You said it. He's speaking as if he's taken sides with the Liberals... Unbelievable.

There's a typical young parliament member, selfishly speaking his mind without considering the context or consequences.

Despite the criticism of his Conservative Party peers, Winston never went against his personal convictions.

Sorry, but this seat is taken.

I see.

Um, this seat is taken, too

It seems you can't find a seat. Perhaps you'd be more comfortable over with the Liberals?

What did you say? I'm a Conservative.

I see. But it appears to us that you belong with the Liberals.

Although an active member of the Conservative Party, the party his father had belonged to, Winston began to feel less aligned with their policy of upholding tradition rather than embracing change and taking new challenges. The final straw came when the Conservatives began urging the support of protective trade. Winston could take no more.

The Conservative Party says we must enforce protective trade to protect our domestic industry as they compete with foreign industry. But I disagree. The reason England has prospered thus far is because of free trade.

What did he just say?

He's completely lost it.

Currently Britain has no foreign threats to its domestic industry. Moreover, government regulation of trade will actually have the effect of restricting economic development.

We're fortunate to have the Liberals, for they advocate free trade.

I have nothing but praise for our friends in the Liberal Party.

Winston remained firm in his beliefs, despite the fact his fellow Conservatives had begun to leave the room.

There's no need for us to listen to this rubbish anymore! Let's go!

What nonsense!

It's time to decide.

In British parliamentary culture, it was very rare for a member to change one's party affiliation. However, Winston changed affiliations from Conservative to Liberal according to his beliefs.

CLAP

CLAP

Welcome aboard!

CLAP

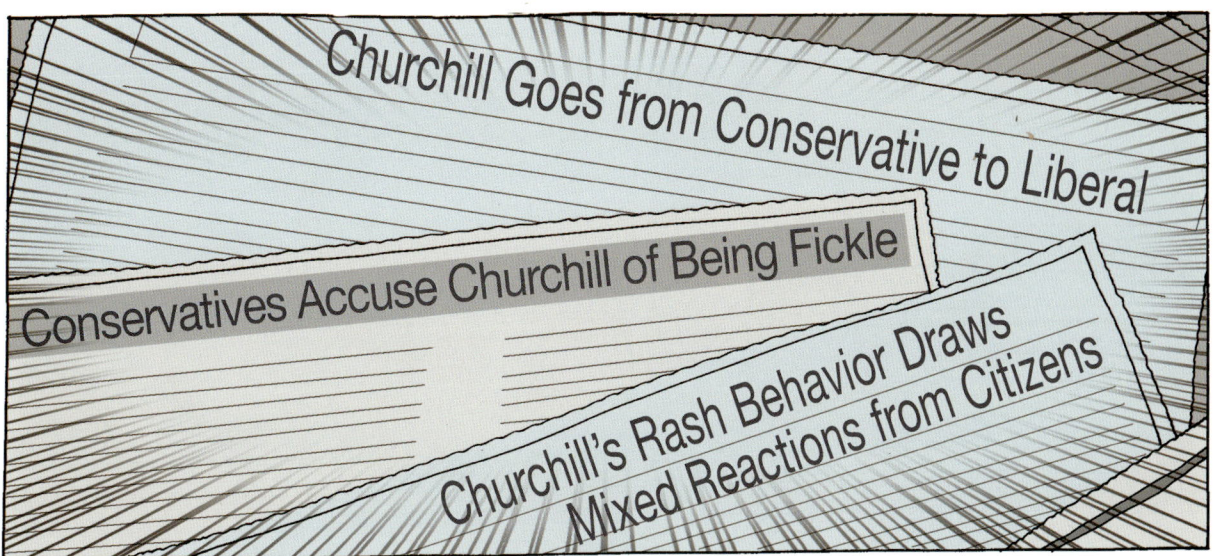

!

Why are all my actions scrutinized so much?

SLAM

Sooner or later the right course of action will become obvious. Appearances aren't everything. As soon as the people can see some concrete results, they'll understand my position.

Around this time Winston met his future wife, Clementine.

Who's that woman? She's beautiful.

Oh, that's Miss Clementine Hozier. She's 23 years old.

It's love at first sight! Miss Clementine!

Oh my!

Owing to Winston's perseverance, he and Clementine were married only six months after meeting at the party.

Two years after getting married and settling down, Winston was appointed to the post of Home Secretary and sent to visit Germany.

Doesn't something seem odd to you?

What is that, sir?

Look at them. Don't they look like they could head off to war any minute?

Um, I suppose so.

Are you saying you think they're preparing for war?

Yes, that's clearly the case. I'm certain war will erupt before long.

Germany is preparing for war. Therefore we must also prepare accordingly.

The military has observed nothing of the sort. Is there any particular reason you believe this to be true, Secretary?

On my trip to Germany I witnessed German soldiers engaging in strict formations and practice drills.

But isn't that simply your conjecture, Secretary? Do you have any real evidence?

It will be too late if we wait until war breaks out to prepare. We too must start increasing troop numbers and produce new weapons.

Why should Germany want to start a war all of a sudden? I think you, Secretary, need to stick to handling domestic affairs and not worry about war.

But...

No! That's enough about this. Please state your view on another topic up for discussion.

Winston's view that England should prepare for war went unsupported. However, once he became First Lord of the Admiralty in 1911, he hastened to prepare England's navy for war.

We've got to increase our troop numbers and supplies.

And we might as well order the newest cannons and faster ships. That's an order!

And just what war are we preparing for, sir?

And what if it's not?

Criticism of your decision to increase the military in peacetime is growing.

They can say what they want. It's clear that war will break out soon. If we're not prepared, we'll suffer great losses to the formidable German army.

Do you think we should let such petty criticism keep us from preventing even greater misfortune later?

No, sir!

In August of 1914, just as Winston had predicted, the world erupted in war.

It's war!

What? Is that true?

Yes, sir! Germany has declared war on France and already attacked Belgium.

It's just as I thought! Ready our forces, quick!

Yes, sir!

As First Lord of the Admiralty, Winston quickly assessed his troop levels and planned a strategy to confront Germany.

It is imperative that we win with as few casualties as possible. To this end, we must prepare a flawless battle plan.

What's the size of our current, combat-ready army?

About seven divisions, sir.

126

After leaving his post as First Lord of Admiralty in the middle of World War I following a strategic failure, Winston was appointed Minister of Munitions, a role in which he fought hard to protect England. On November 11, 1918, after a great number of casualties, World War I ended in victory by the Allied Powers.

07 .The Great War Leader

 Track 20 ▶

The aftermath of World War I was severe. Germany, which had accepted all responsibility for the war through the Treaty of Versailles, was in a bad state, with its citizens struggling just to make a living.

This is all I have to sell today.

I've got money. Sell it to me!

I was first!

But the price is double.

Double?! How can the price double overnight?

These items are made for export to repay war debts. And I don't have many to begin with.

This is the painful price we pay for losing the war.

What's the use of working so hard? It's a hopeless situation where everybody's having trouble getting by.

The Germans lost hope in the tough post-war times. It was in such a social environment that Nazi leader Adolf Hitler became chancellor of Germany.

There is no hope for Germany if we continue on the present path. Your lives will not improve regardless of your effort!

For Germany to prosper, it must unify its scattered race. To do this, we must be prepared for war!

The master German race can lead the world! Ladies and gentlemen, the time has come to work together!

Hitler! Hitler!

Yeah!

The war is over. To heal our wounds as quickly as possible, we must send our youth home to their families.

I disagree. How can you be sure that war won't erupt again?

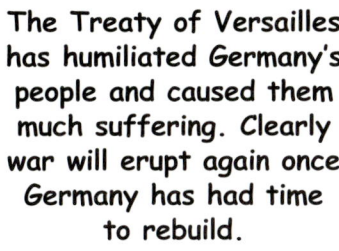

The Treaty of Versailles has humiliated Germany's people and caused them much suffering. Clearly war will erupt again once Germany has had time to rebuild.

Right now the Germans are having a hard enough time just getting by day to day. They don't have the strength to start another war.

But the very ambitious Hitler has become chancellor. He's the one who will start a war.

It's time to expel warmonger Churchill from Parliament!

We won't stand for war!

No war when we've finally got peace!

War will sacrifice even more of our young!

WARMONGER CHURCHILL!

CHURCHILL. RESIGN!

What!

No more war!

Why do they only think in the short term? Hitler could start a war any day now.

If war were to break out now, there would be untold suffering.

Nobody will listen to me!

Giving up is not your style. They will listen to you eventually.

Just as Winston predicted, before long Hitler violated the Treaty of Versailles and stationed his army in the demilitarized zone of Rheinland.

Next is Czechoslovakia!

Heil Hitler!

To unify the German race, Hitler first annexed the country of Austria and then set his sights on the Sudeten Region of Czechoslovakia.

Please support the annexation of the Sudetenland, where many ethnic Germans live.

As for England, we and France support the annexation of Sudetenland with Germany if it will prevent war.

How foolish can you be to recognize the annexation of Sudetenland with Germany?

That's the same as surrendering without even putting up a fight. This decision will haunt us for many years to come.

What are you saying?

Is that Churchill again?

Can you rest assured that war will not erupt tomorrow? This is not the time to avoid war, but the time to face it head on.

Go ahead, call me a warmonger! Germany said it only wanted to annex the Sudetenland, but look at it now. We're on the brink of war, and we can't just sit and watch.

Hmm.

Just think of how our young soldiers will suffer fighting a war they are not prepared to fight!

He's got a point.

Recent world events indicate that things are turning out just as Churchill warned.

Early on the morning of September 1, 1939, just as Germany was invading Poland, Winston was once again appointed First Lord of the Admiralty.

Good to have you back, sir.

Thank you. England needs me, and I shall do my best.

I want to get started right away, so I'll need an update on the current state of affairs.

Hitler's German army has crossed Poland, Belgium, and Luxembourg, and is now advancing toward France.

This is serious. If Hitler manages to invade France, then England will no longer be safe.

War is imminent.

On September 3, 1939, England and France declared war on Germany. The world was once again swept into war.

The combined forces of England and France fought fiercely against the German army.

But Germany's army was very strong. Before long it had conquered both the Netherlands and Belgium.

The world was in a state of confusion by the unexpected events of World War II. For England to emerge victorious, a leader like Winston Churchill was necessary.

Your Royal Highness, I do not have the ability to lead our country to victory in war. I hereby step down from office.

Have you thought about a successor?

Yes. Winston Churchill.

Isn't he currently First Lord of the Admiralty? Won't it be difficult for him to immediately assume the office of Prime Minister?

The people of Britain want him to be Prime Minister.

Churchill predicted this war and insisted we prepare for it. He does not lack ability.

Hmm, I see.

I'm sure you're aware of the current worsening situation. I trust you can win back the trust of our citizens.

I'll do my best.

Congratulations on becoming Prime Minister, sir.

It will be difficult in this time of war.

I don't see it that way.

I'm actually relieved to have become Prime Minister in such difficult times. I'm grateful to England for choosing me to lead them in this time of peril. I just hope it's not too late.

Prime Minister!

Three days after becoming Prime Minister, Winston addressed the nation for the first time.

Mommy, if war starts will you and Daddy have to separate?

I sure hope not.

Mommy, who is that?

That is...

I have nothing to offer but blood, toil, tears, and sweat.

We have before us an ordeal of the most grievous kind. We have before us many, many long months of struggle and of suffering. You ask, what is our policy?

I can say, it is to wage war, by sea, land, and air...

!

...with all our might and with all the strength that God can give us; to wage war against a monstrous tyranny, never surpassed in the dark, lamentable catalogue of human crime. That is our policy!

You ask, what is our aim? I can answer in one word. It is victory, victory at all costs, victory in spite of all terror, victory, however long and hard the road may be!

HOORAY!

YEAH!

Dear, we're going to win! Prime Minister Churchill will make sure we win the war!

The British and French armies fought the Germans fiercely in Belgium, but Germany overran both armies, isolating them along the northern French coast of Dunkirk,

If we continue on this course the Allied forces will be wiped out. We must have them escape to Britain.

But don't we need more ships? If the Allied forces are to escape, they're going to have to abandon their weapons.

Even so, would you rather them stay and be destroyed?

We'll be at a disadvantage with fewer weapons, but we can't disregard the valuable lives of our soldiers. Give the order to escape.

The Allied forces safely escaped, but the situation worsened.

Attention, everyone! Apparently Germany has taken control of France.

What? France too?

Almost every country in Europe has fallen into the hands of Germany.

Can we really win this war?

We should surrender before we suffer additional losses.

Now England is completely isolated. Moreover, with hardly any weapons what other option do we have?

Your Lordship, please make your decision!

Hitler clearly expects us to concede peacefully to his forces.

But Britain is the only country left that can stand up to Germany.

146

If we stand up to Germany and win, the world will once again be free, but if we concede defeat the world will enter an age of darkness.

The hope of the world rests with Britain.

We have no choice but to win. A win for England is a win for the world.

We have to fight to the end!

Let's fight!

Believe in Britain!

The instant Britain refused to surrender, Germany attacked. Hitler ordered bombing raids because Britain was an island country surrounded by water.

A missile has hit your official residence, Prime Minister.

You must take cover at once.

I'm just fine.

No! My duty is to usher you to a safe location.

Do you really think I'm going to run away after a few little bombs? That's absurd!

But the situation is very dangerous.

I'm not the only one standing unarmed against Germany's artillery fire. They're all counting on me to fight to the end.

Knowing that, there's no way I can think only of my own safety!

149

It's the Prime Minister.

Churchill.

It will take the effort and pain of countless people to rebuild this city

What brought you here, sir?

It is dangerous to stay here. We could be bombed again any minute.

But don't you all live here?

Yes, but Prime Minister, all the hope of Britain rests with you, not us.

Wrong. Every life is precious.

Please be patient a little longer.

I'm doing my best to see that this war ends as quickly as possible.

150

08 Leaving One's Mark in History

 Track 32 ▶

Despite Germany's merciless attacks, Britain did not surrender. Through secret negotiations with President Roosevelt of the United States, Britain received additional war supplies.

In December of 1941, Japan bombed the U.S. territory of Pearl Harbor, Hawaii. The U.S. immediately declared war on Japan, and the Pacific War began.

Then, in April, 1945, after untold casualties on all sides, World War II ended following Germany's defeat at the hands of the U.S. and the Soviet Union.

England had another election soon after Germany surrendered defeat. Winston was confident he would be reelected after his meritorious performance during the war.

My work is not yet finished. I've got to ensure that this war ends in complete victory.

We must prepare well for my electoral address to the people.

Yes, sir!

The fact that there's going to be a general election even before the war has completely ended tells me the Labour Party is short on new ideas.

No Socialist government conducting the entire life and industry of the country could afford to allow free expressions of public discontent.

ON AIR

The socialism-supporting Labour Party would have to fall back on some form of Gestapo*.

Did he just compare the Labour Party to the Gestapo? He better watch his language!

*Gestapo: The abbreviation of Geheime Staatspolizei, or Secret State Police, the Gestapo was the official secret police of Nazi Germany. The Gestapo was notorious for its oppression of communism and socialism, and for atrocities committed against Jews, including purging and genocide.

However, the Conservative Party respects England's idea of freedom.

Isn't the Gestapo that secret Nazi police?

I don't care how much you disagree with the Labour Party's policies comparing them to the enemy's police is going too far!

You can't go around making such accusations so soon after war has ended.

This brings back grim memories of war.

This is our chance! The Labour Party can make use of Churchill's poor choice of words and emerge victorious.

Ladies and gentlemen, a few minutes ago I believe you had the chance to vividly hear the speech of an impatient and intolerant politician, Winston Churchill.

Churchill was an excellent wartime leader, but now the situation is completely different.

What, what is he saying?

What Britain needs now is a government and leader that can sort out the aftermath of war!

He's right. The war's over.

It's time for Churchill to step aside.

The election ended with the Labour Party returning to power. Winston was taken by complete surprise.

The Labour Party has formed a majority government after getting an overwhelming number of votes in the election!

I-I can't believe it!

It's a complete loss for the Conservative Party.

In July, 1945, Churchill accepted the will of his countrymen and left the office of Prime Minister.

Let's leave now.

Yes, sir.

After losing the election, Winston left politics. He spent his free time painting and writing.

Whew, this isn't easy, either.

Is this the way it's supposed to end?

Is there no place that requires my service?

Winston began writing books describing his experiences with war and politics, and his political convictions.

What are you writing about?

I'm writing about war, about the shocking experiences I had when I first entered the battlefield. It was more wretched and horrible than anything you can imagine.

Back then, I couldn't appreciate why we went to war, or for whom all those innocent lives were being sacrificed.

So did you find the answers?

I thought I could find the answers by becoming a member of Parliament. But even after becoming Prime Minister, the answers still elude me.

However, the one thing I'm sure of is that such a war must never happen again. I hope others can read about my experiences and learn the lessons taught by war.

I sure hope so.

Looking back on his life, Winston focused all his efforts on collecting materials to write a memoir of World War II.

1953 was a great year for Winston. He won the Nobel Prize in Literature for his memoir, *The Second World War*.

Is it true Churchill got the Nobel Prize for his book?

Yep, I came to the bookstore as soon as I heard the news.

You say it sold over 200,000 copies in one day?

Seeing this book brings back memories of the war.

It seems like it all happened so long ago.

Back then, Britain was in no position to win the war.

Right. Germany seemed unstoppable, and I was sure we didn't have a chance of winning.

Yes! But after hearing Churchill's speech we started believing we could be victorious.

After hearing him speak I wanted to run outside and offer myself to the war cause.

His words really were powerful back then.

162

That same year, Winston was also knighted. The queen made him a knight of the Order of the Garter, which was Britain's highest order of knighthood.

I hereby raise Winston Churchill to Knight of the Order of the Garter, in recognition of his distinguished service to Britain. I will now refer to you as Sir Winston Churchill.

I am honored, Your Majesty the Queen.

However, such happy times were short-lived. The increasingly frail Winston soon suffered a stroke.

Uh.

Dear!

His condition is not good. Part of his body has become paralyzed, rendering him unable to talk.

Oh, dear!

On January 24, 1965, the 70th anniversary of his father Randolph Winston's death, a cold winter rain was falling outside.

My mind hasn't felt this clear in a long time.

Clementine,

you're so beautiful even after all these years. I know being with me was not easy... I just want you to know I thank you, and that I'm sorry.

Now that I think of it, today's the anniversary of my father's death. I feel like he's standing right beside me.

164

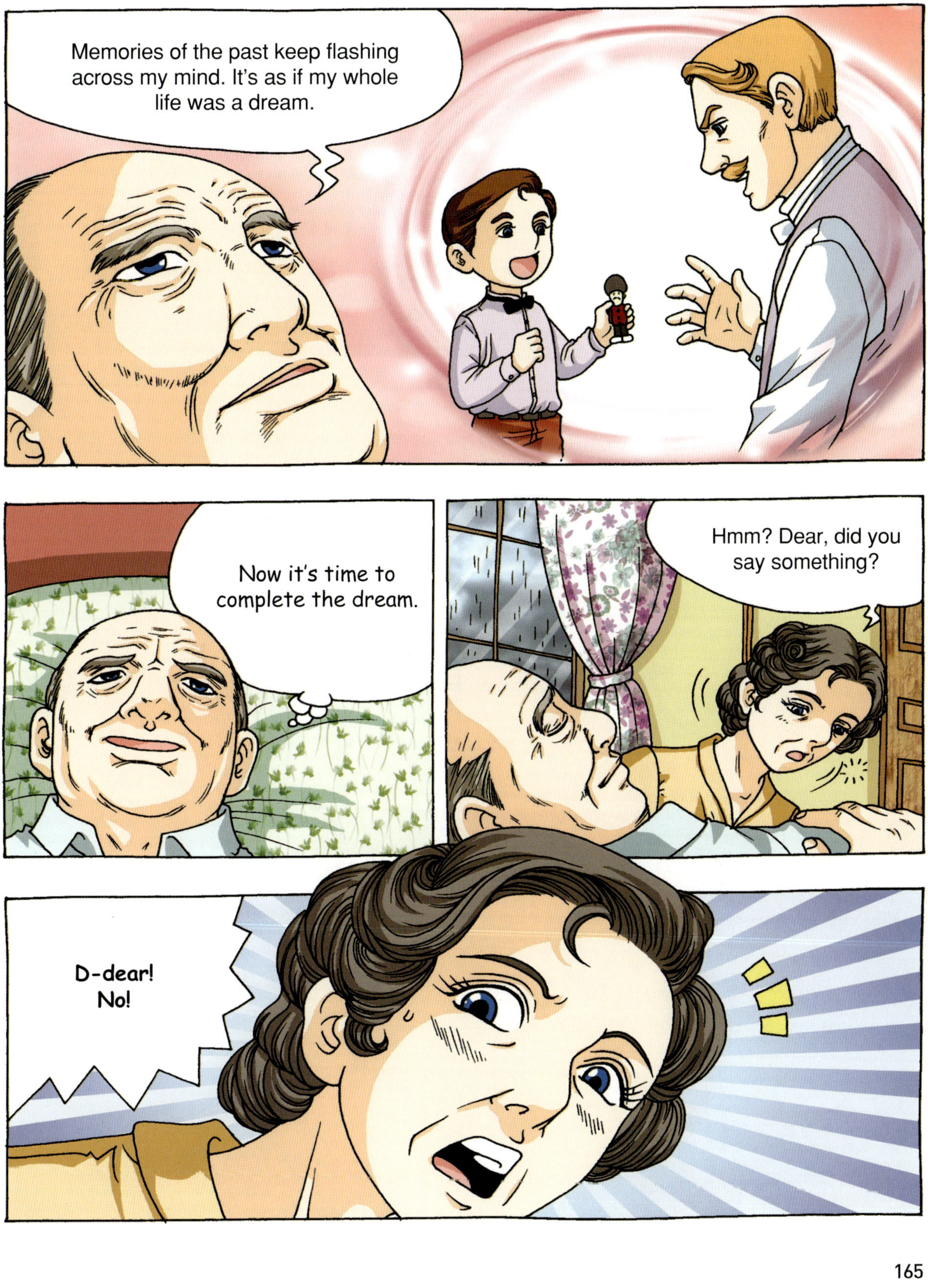

Memories of the past keep flashing across my mind. It's as if my whole life was a dream.

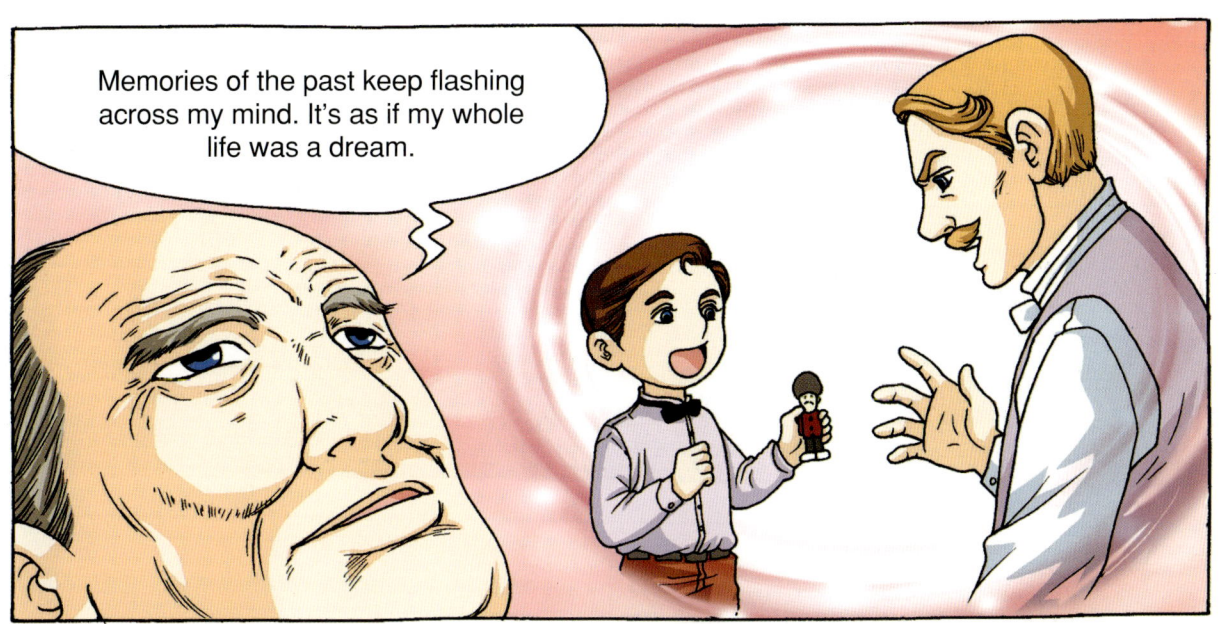

Now it's time to complete the dream.

Hmm? Dear, did you say something?

D-dear! No!

A radio news flash announced Winston's passing, and all of England became overwhelmed with grief.

Son, do you know what kind of man Winston Churchill was?

Yes! Churchill was a great man who saved Britain.

Right, and not only Britain, he saved all countries that respect freedom.

We've lost a great leader.

It was a very cold day in England. The cold, biting wind was freezing the arms and legs of those waiting outside.

Despite the freezing cold, great numbers of people lined up to pay their last respects to Winston.

Our family owes everything to you. Please rest in peace.

To mourn its national hero, all flags across England were flown at half-mast, while the Westminster Palace clock was paused.

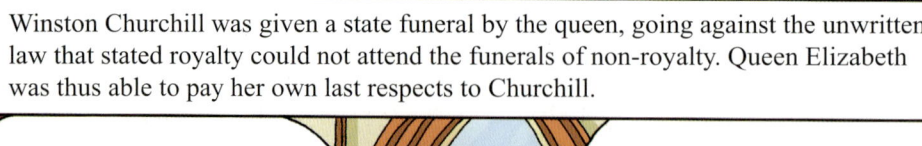

Winston Churchill was given a state funeral by the queen, going against the unwritten law that stated royalty could not attend the funerals of non-royalty. Queen Elizabeth was thus able to pay her own last respects to Churchill.

I extend my condolences to a leader who had keen insight into the future and unyielding courage.

Sir Winston Churchill was the reason Britain and the other Allied Powers were victorious in war.

He was a champion of freedom who never lost his composure.

England wasn't the only country in mourning. People all around the world watched the televised funeral and paid their last respects to a hero who had lived almost a century.

Although Churchill led a solitary life fighting for freedom, at the end of his life he was anything but alone. The world was there to say goodbye.

As Winston had requested, he was buried in his family's plot at a church in Oxfordshire. Winston did not consider himself to be special. On the contrary, as a man with many weaknesses, he learned how to overcome those weaknesses while never compromising his beliefs, no matter how severely he was criticized. Once he decided on a course of action, he steadfastly pursued it until he succeeded. As a result, he became a hero who saved Britain and the rest of Europe in World War II.

If there had been no Winston Churchill, not only England, but also the entire world would have turned out much differently. He will be remembered forever as a great leader who won the trust of his countrymen through his charismatic oratory and courageously stood up to Germany.

Lesson **1**

Word Search

● Find the words which are hidden horizontally, vertically and diagonally.

```
Q M Z P R A N K S T E R Q Q M Z G Q M T
W S I U V E N T I O N H W W N A H W N O
E B Q J A B Q J E T B A D M I R E O B M
R V C K R D C K R V C K R R V C K P V M
E C A O R S E N T C D L T T C D U G C E
V O E Q Y X E O Y X E Q Y Y X E N O X M
E U V W U D V W C Z V W R U Z V J R Z W
A R A E I A E E I A R E E I A R A T A C
L A I R O S G C O S T R C O S G S U S O
P G C S P E R S E V E R A N C E T N D M
A E A Y H F U Y A T U Y V A F U Y I F P
S G S U E T I N C R I G E I N G U T G R
D H S I D S M I D H O I R D H O I Y H O
F J A B S O C A F J T J F F J T J F J M
G K N B G K R A R E P M E M O I R G K I
H L A N H L E N P E E N H H L E N H L S
J Q T M J Q T A U E D O R I T Y M J B E
L W E Q L W Y Q L W Y Q L L W Y Q L U Y
Z W K F Z W K F Z W K F Z Z S U F T G R
X E M I L I T A R Y I P A L E M U X N M
C R Q C C R Q C P C I G H T R Q C C R Q
```

prankster	courage	military	admire
perseverance	escape	compromise	memoir

Vocabulary

● Match each word to the correct meaning.

1. affiliation   • 발음

2. politicians   • 일을 계속하다

3. hellion   • 가입

4. work on   • 발음

5. pronunciation   • 망나니

6. patience   • 전쟁

7. persuasive   • 끈기

8. war   • 설득력이 있는

9. war correspondent   • 악몽

10. nightmare   • 종군기자

11. parliament   • 수상, 국무총리

12. prime minister   • 의회

Guess What?

● Guess what he said in the blank.

Darn!

So I'm stupid because I stammer?

Just wait!

Winston read books out loud in front of a mirror to improve his pronunciation.

Had t-t-ta en his last l-l-love, no, leave, of the w-w-weeping m-morn,

R-r-rose-ch-ch-cheeked Adonis hied him to the ch-ch-chase, h-h-hunting he loved.

Wow, is it already morning?

The Blitz

This is a picture of London in the Blitz, Nazi bombing raids during World War II(1939~1945). It has been estimated that about 40,000 civilians were killed, 46,000 injured, and more than a million homes destroyed in the horrible Blitz by the Nazis. Write verbs, nouns, adjectives describing the picture.

Verbs	Adjectives	Nouns
destroy	cruel	disaster

About Anne Frank

Anne Frank(1929~1945) is probably the most famous Jewish girl in the world since World War II. Even though She did not survive the 'Holocaust' which refers to Nazi genocide program of systematically killing Jewish people in Nazi territories, but she left her secret diary documenting two and a half years in hiding, depicting a girl's pure mind and hope amid ugly cruel war time. The rare and touching diary of Anne Frank is one of the most widely read pieces of non-fiction up to now.

▲ Write a diary which includes some international news or social events along with your personal daily life, feelings, opinions, and hopes. Diaries can be precious historial records and literary pieces.

Dear Diary,   **Date :**

Quizzes

● Choose the best answers for the blanks.

1. When Winston Churchill was a child, his parents _____.

   a. adored him   b. were proud of him   c. neglected him

2. During his childhood, the teachers at the boarding school thought, he was _____.

   a. a naughty boy   b. a smart boy   c. a genius

3. He served as prime minister _____.

   a. once   b. twice   c. three times

4. He wrote _____.

   a. *The World Crisis*   b. *The World History*   c. *The World War*

5. In 1953 he won the _____.

   a. Nobel Prize in Literature   b. Pulitzer Prize   c. Academy Award

6. His trademark was his _____.

   a. smile   b. military uniform   c. cigar and V sign

7. The alliance of Britain, France and Russia was called the _____.

   a. Angels   b. Allies   c. Axis

8. The German dictator during World War II was _____.

   a. Berito Mussolini   b. Joseph Stalin   c. Adolf Hitler

9. German members of Adolf Hitler's political party were called _____.

   a. Nazis   b. Nemo   c. Nabi

10. A war in which Britain, France , the Soviet Union, the United States, China and other allies defeated Germany, Italy, and Japan from 1939 to 1945 known as _____.

    a. World War II   b. World War I   c. Civil War

Answers : 1-c, 2-a, 3-b, 4-a, 5-a, 6-c, 7-b, 8-c, 9-a, 10-b

연표

1874년 11월 30일, 영국 옥스퍼드셔 주에서 태어났습니다.

1882년 08세 성 조지 학교에 입학합니다.

1884년 10세 브라이튼의 예비학교로 전학합니다.

1893년 19세 샌드허스트 육군사관학교에 입학합니다.

1895년 21세 샌드허스트 육군관학교를 졸업하고 제4경기병 연대에 입대합니다.

1899년 25세 『모닝포스트』지의 종군 기자로 보어 전쟁에 참가합니다.
보어군에게 포로로 잡혔다가 탈출에 성공하여 국민적 영웅이 됩니다.

1900년 26세 보수당의 후보로 출마하여 하원 의원에 당선됩니다.

1904년 30세 보수당의 정책에 반대하여 자유당으로 옮깁니다.

1906년 32세 『랜돌프 처칠 경』을 씁니다.

1908년 34세 클레멘타인 호지에와 결혼합니다.

1910년 36세 내무 장관으로 취임합니다.

1911년 37세 해군 장관이 됩니다.

1915년 41세 제1차 세계 대전 중 작전 실패의 책임을 지고
              해군 장관에서 물러납니다.

1917년 43세 군수 장관에 임명됩니다.

1919년 45세 육군 장관 겸 공군 장관이 됩니다.

1921년 47세 식민 장관이 됩니다.

1939년 65세 해군 장관으로 복귀합니다.

1940년 66세 총리에 취임합니다.

1951년 77세 총리에 다시 취임합니다.

1953년 79세 기사 작위와 가터 훈장을 받습니다.
              『제2차 세계 대전』으로 노벨문학상을 수상합니다.

1965년 91세 1월 24일, 세상을 떠납니다. 국장으로 장례식이 치러집니다.

Note

Biography Comic who?

who? 01	Barack Obama	979-11-5639-023-7
who? 02	Charles Darwin	979-11-5639-024-4
who? 03	Bill Gates	979-11-5639-025-1
who? 04	Hillary Clinton	979-11-5639-026-8
who? 05	Stephen Hawking	979-11-5639-027-5
who? 06	Oprah Winfrey	979-11-5639-028-2
who? 07	Steven Spielberg	979-11-5639-029-9
who? 08	Thomas Edison	979-11-5639-030-5
who? 09	Abraham Lincoln	979-11-5639-031-2
who? 10	Martin Luther King, Jr.	979-11-5639-032-9
who? 11	Louis Braille	979-11-5639-033-6
who? 12	Albert Einstein	979-11-5639-034-3
who? 13	Jane Goodall	979-11-5639-035-0
who? 14	Walt Disney	979-11-5639-036-7
who? 15	Winston Churchill	979-11-5639-037-4
who? 16	Warren Buffett	979-11-5639-008-4
who? 17	Nelson Mandela	979-11-5639-009-1
who? 18	Steve Jobs	979-11-5639-010-7
who? 19	J. K. Rowling	979-11-5639-011-4
who? 20	Jean-Henri Fabre	979-11-5639-012-1
who? 21	Vincent van Gogh	979-11-5639-013-8
who? 22	Marie Curie	979-11-5639-014-5
who? 23	Henry David Thoreau	979-11-5639-015-2
who? 24	Andrew Carnegie	979-11-5639-016-9
who? 25	Coco Chanel	979-11-5639-017-6
who? 26	Charlie Chaplin	979-11-5639-018-3
who? 27	Ho Chi Minh	979-11-5639-019-0
who? 28	Ludwig van Beethoven	979-11-5639-020-6
who? 29	Mao Zedong	979-11-5639-021-3
who? 30	Kim Dae-jung	979-11-5639-022-0